Oxford Levels
Placement and
Progress Kit

Workbook 4

This book belongs to:

_____

Activities by Karra McFarlane
Series created by Roderick Hunt and Alex Brychta

OXFORD
UNIVERSITY PRESS

OXFORD
UNIVERSITY PRESS

Great Clarendon Street, Oxford, OX2 6DP, United Kingdom

Oxford University Press is a department of the University of Oxford. It furthers the University's objective of excellence in research, scholarship, and education by publishing worldwide. Oxford is a registered trade mark of Oxford University Press in the UK and in certain other countries

British Library Cataloguing in Publication Data

Data available

ISBN: 978-0-1984-4519-7

10 9 8 7 6 5 4 3 2

Paper used in the production of this book is a natural, recyclable product made from wood grown in sustainable forests. The manufacturing process conforms to the environmental regulations of the country of origin.

Printed in China by Golden Cup Printing Co Ltd

Acknowledgements

Series consultant: Catherine Baker

Activities by: Karra McFarlane

The publisher would like to thank the following for permission to reproduce photographs: **p34**: www.BibleLandPictures.com/Alamy Stock Photo; **p36**: Spain, Barcelona, Parc Guell. Chocolate House/Omniphoto/UIG/Bridgeman Images; **p37**: Yiu Tung Lee/Dreamstime; **p45(l)**: drnadig/Getty Images; **p54**: Jacques Langevin/Sygma/Sygma via Getty Images; **p55(t)**: RubberBall/Alamy Stock Photo; **p55(b)**: Jon Bower Japan/Alamy Stock Photo; **p57(t)**: AF archive/Alamy Stock Photo; **p57(b)**: Fernando Quevedo de Oliveira/Alamy Stock Photo. All other photos by Shutterstock. ***Mosaic Art* front cover**: Felix Lipov/Shutterstock.com; Repina Valeriya/Shuttertock; Elenamiv/Shutterstock; ***Mosaic Art* back cover**: A_Lesik/Shutterstock; ***Plants for Dinner* cover**: Bildagentur Zoonar GmbH/Shutterstock; bergamont/Shutterstock; ***Dressing Up* cover**: windmoon/Shutterstock.com; Alvin Ganesh/Shutterstock; vlad09/Shutterstock

Contents Page

Tick the books you have finished.

The Stars

1 Why was it a good night to look at the stars?
Tick the correct answer.

☐ The moon was very bright.

☐ It was a clear night.

☐ The sun was still out.

2 When does the story take place?
Circle the correct answer.

at night-time

in the middle of the day

early in the morning

3 Why did Gran and the children go to the top of the hill to look at the stars?
Tick the correct answer.

☐ There was a good view of the sky.

☐ It was too windy in the garden.

☐ The moon was brighter there.

4 Look at page 9.

Colour the group of stars called the Big Dipper.

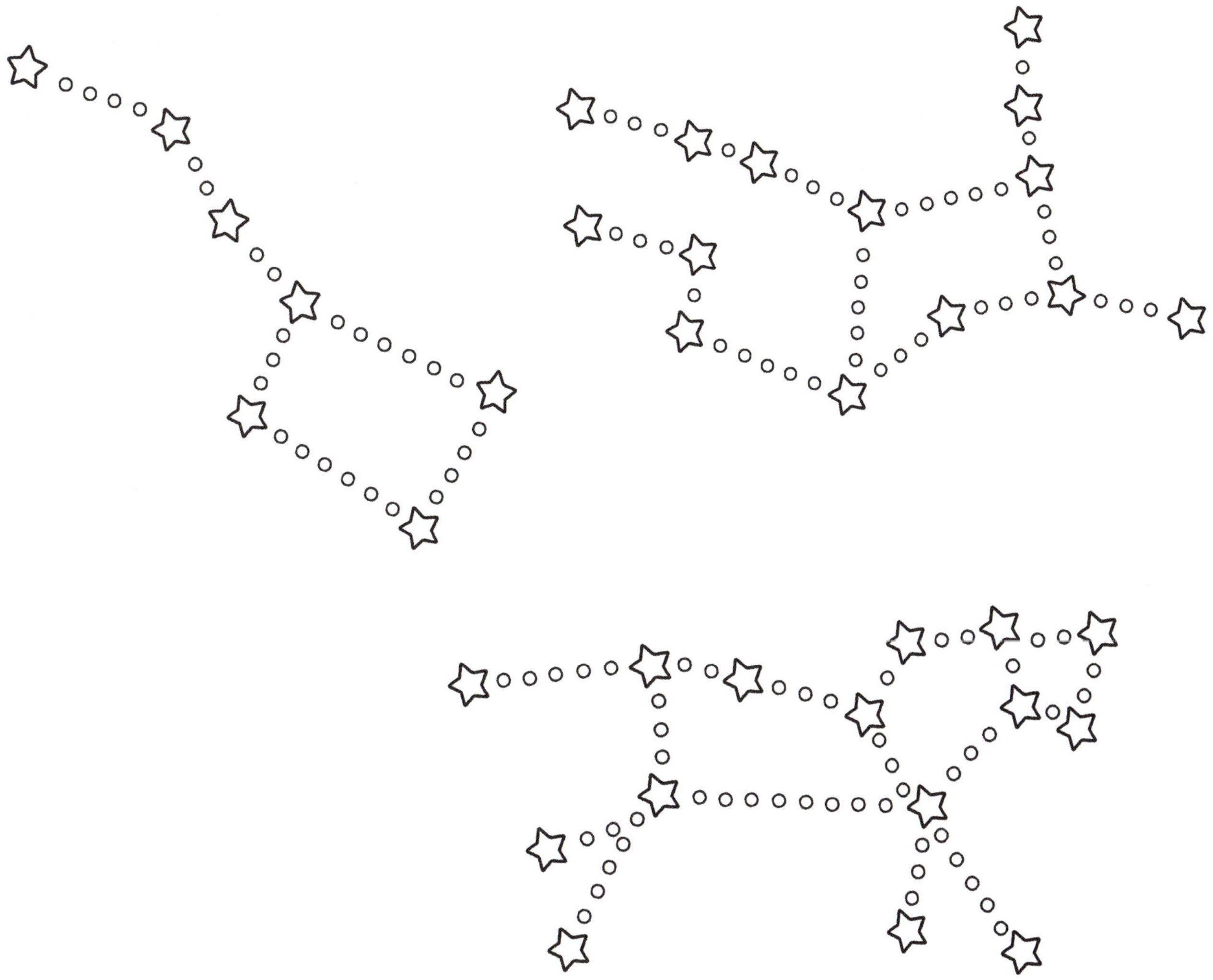

5 Look at page 10. **"Look, there it is!"**

Why has the author used an exclamation mark (!) here?

Tick the correct answer.

 to show Chip is cross with Biff

to show Chip is joking

 to show Chip is excited to see the Big Dipper

6 Which of these is a group of two stars?
Tick the correct answer.

☐ the Lion

☐ the Twins

☐ the Big Dipper

7 Look at pages 12 to 13.
Write the missing word to complete this sentence.

When Gran said **the Little Dog**, Floppy looked at

the _____.

| sky | map | moon |

8 **"And there's the big dog!" said Biff.**
Why does Biff call Floppy **the big dog**?
Tick the correct answer.

☐ Floppy usually looks much smaller.

☐ Floppy is a very small dog.

☐ Biff is making a joke.

9 Which words have the same meaning?
Draw lines to match the words.

bright

little

big

massive

shining

small

10 Put the pictures from the story in order.
Write numbers 1, 2 and 3 in the boxes to show the
order that they happened.

11 How much did you enjoy the story and activities?
Colour one face to show how you feel.

12 Draw a picture of a group of stars from the story.
Label the group of stars you have drawn.

Book word count: 157

Long Legs

1 Which word describes the clowns?
Circle the correct word.

| short | huge | tiny |

2 **"What big feet!" said Kipper. "What long legs!"**
Write the missing word to complete this sentence.

The author uses exclamation marks to show that

Kipper is _____.

| angry | sad | surprised |

3 What did the clown in the green jacket juggle with?
Circle the correct picture.

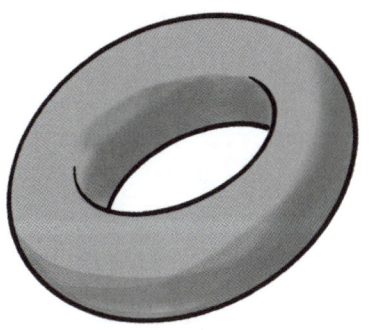  

4 **"We will need long legs to get it down," said Kipper.**

Why did Kipper say they need *long legs* to get Dad's hat?

Tick the correct answer.

☐ The hat was up high.

☐ The hat had blown under a car.

☐ He was too tall to reach the hat.

5 How did Kipper try to reach the hat first?
Circle the correct answer.

He stood on his tiptoes.   He sat on Dad's back.

He jumped up high.

6 Why did Kipper ask the clowns to get Dad's hat?
Tick the correct answer.

☐ They ran quickly.

☐ They jumped high.

☐ They were tall.

7 Which words have opposite meanings?
Draw lines to match the words.

up

low

tall

short

high

down

8 Look at page 16.
How did Kipper feel when he was on the clown's back?
Circle the correct word.

worried

excited

happy

9 Put the pictures from the story in order.
Write numbers 1, 2 and 3 in the boxes to show the
order that they happened.

10 Choose a new title for this story.
Tick the best answer.

☐ Kipper and the Clowns to the Rescue

☐ Short Legs

☐ Dad Saves his Favourite Hat

11 How much did you enjoy the story and activities? Colour one face to show how you feel.

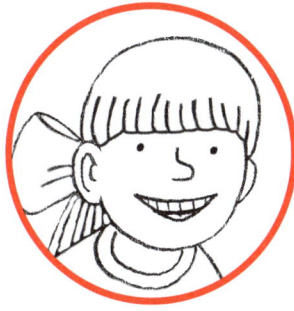

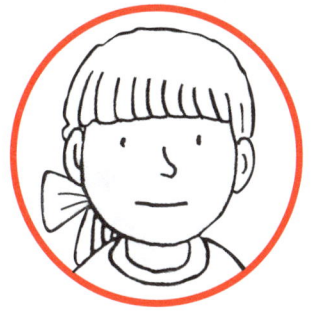

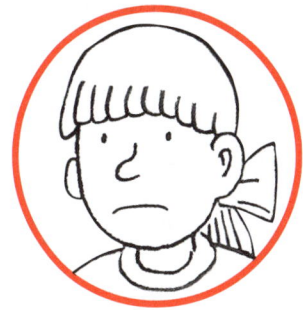

12 Draw some things for the clown to juggle with. Write the names of the things below.

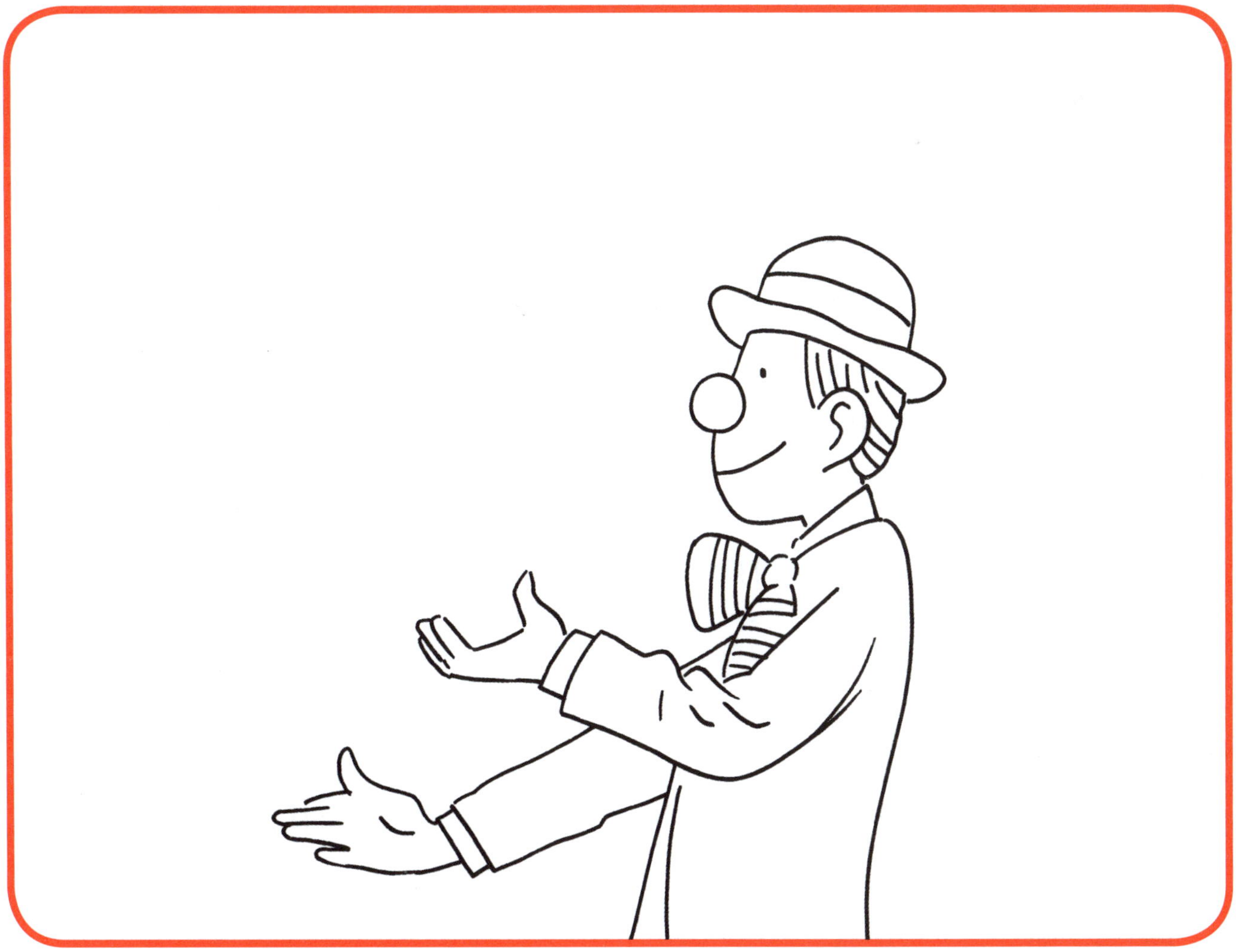

____

____

Book word count: 184

The Seal Pup

1 What did Mum think the seal's mother was doing?
Circle the correct answer.

getting help   getting food

sunbathing

2 Look at page 3.
Why was Biff worried about the seal?
Tick the correct answer.

☐ She thought it might be stuck.

☐ She thought it might be lost.

☐ She thought it might be hurt.

3 Look at page 3.
Which punctuation mark shows us that Biff is asking
a question?
Circle the correct answer.

.   ?   "

4 What happened before Dad sent for help?
Tick the correct answer.

☐ The family waited to see if the seal's mother came back.

☐ The family tried to move the seal.

☐ The family called out for the seal's mother.

5 How did the Seal Rescue Team get the seal on to the boat?
Circle the correct answer.

They chased it.

They tricked it.

They lifted it together.

6 Write the missing word to complete the sentence.

angry   sick   happy

Mrs Hill was glad Dad called the Seal Rescue Team

because the seal was _____.

7 Look at page 12.
Write the missing word to complete this sentence.

When the family went to see the seal, he

was _____.

tired   healthy   unwell

8 Why did the Seal Rescue Team take the seal back to the sea?
Tick the correct answer.

☐ There was not enough room for him.

☐ They had found the seal's mother.

☐ The seal had grown and was well.

9 Circle the word that shows us the sound the seal made in the sea.

saying   splash   goodbye

10 Put the pictures from the story in order.
Write numbers 1, 2 and 3 in the boxes to show the order that they happened.

11 How much did you enjoy the story and activities?
Colour one face to show how you feel.

12 Draw a picture of the seal and his mother.
Label your picture with the name of the seal.

Book word count: 181

Floppy and the Skateboard

1 Look at page 3.
Which word means the same as *fantastic*?
Circle the correct word.

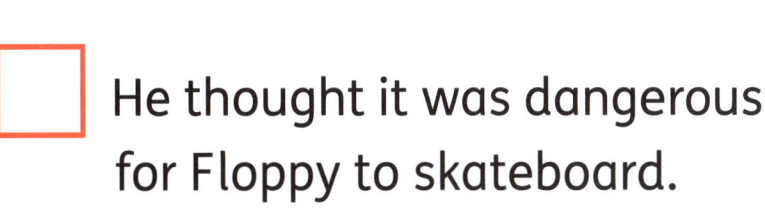

terrible   boring   brilliant

2 Look at page 8.
Why did Wilf shout "**No, Floppy!**" here?
Tick the correct answer.

☐ He thought it was dangerous
for Floppy to skateboard.

☐ He did not want Floppy to have any fun.

☐ He did not want anyone to use his skateboard.

3 Which word describes Floppy skateboarding down
the hill?
Circle the correct word.

slow   quick

steady

4 Look at pages 8 to 9.
Why was Floppy going so fast?
Tick the correct answer.

☐ He was skateboarding up a hill.

☐ Wilf's skateboard was new.

☐ He was skateboarding down a hill.

5 Put the characters in the order they chased after Floppy.
Write numbers 1, 2 and 3 in the correct boxes.

Biff and Chip
☐

Wilf
☐

Wilf's mum
☐

6 Write the missing word to complete this sentence.

Wilf's mum could not catch Floppy because he was

going too _____.

| slowly | fast | carefully |

7 Look at page 13.
Why did Wilf's dad drop the ice creams?
Tick the correct answer.

☐ He was worried about Floppy so he was running after him.

☐ He did not want them any more.

☐ They were too cold to hold.

8 What stopped Floppy in the end?
Circle the correct answer.

| a tree | a duck | the pond |

9 Write the missing word to complete this sentence.

The author wrote **Good trick, Floppy!** at the end of

the story to make you _____.

| laugh | worry | stop |

10 Put the events from the story in order.
Write numbers 1, 2 and 3 in the boxes to show the
order that they happened.

☐ Floppy fell into the pond.

☐ Floppy jumped on to Wilf's skateboard and
rolled away.

☐ Biff, Chip and Wilf did tricks on their
skateboards.

11 How much did you enjoy the story and activities?
Colour one face to show how you feel.

12 Design your own skateboard.
Write a list of words to describe your skateboard.

_____

_____

Gran's New Glasses

1 What was Gran painting?
Tick the correct answer.

☐ the shelf

☐ the window

☐ the gate

2 Look at page 4. **But it was not level.**
What does *level* mean?
Circle the correct word.

wobbly　　　　solid　　　　straight

3 How did Chip know that Gran could not see very well?
Tick the correct answer.

☐ Gran put the pizza upside down on the plate.

☐ Gran lost her glasses.

☐ Gran gave them pizza for dinner.

4 Put the pictures from the story in order.
Write numbers 1, 2 and 3 in the boxes to show the
order that they happened.

☐ ☐ ☐

5 Look at pages 12 to 13.
What did Biff, Chip and Mum think of the glasses Gran
tried on?
Tick the correct answer.

☐ They loved them.

☐ They thought they made her look younger.

☐ They did not like them.

6 Look at pages 12 to 13.
Write the missing word to complete this sentence.

| yes | Gran | no |

The author uses the word _____ lots of times to

show that Biff, Chip and Mum don't like the glasses.

7 Put the glasses in the order that Gran tried them on.
Write numbers 1, 2 and 3 in the correct boxes.

8 Which glasses did Gran think were the best?
Circle the correct answer.

| her old glasses | the glasses with stars on |

| some sunglasses |

9 Look at page 16. **"My old pair … with new lenses."**
What are **lenses**?
Tick the correct answer.

☐ the frame around glasses

☐ the glass inside glasses

☐ the colour of glasses

10 Look at page 16.
Write the missing word to complete the sentence.

hated

disliked

liked

Mum _____ the glasses Gran picked at the

end of the story.

11 How much did you enjoy the story and activities? Colour one face to show how you feel.

12 Design a new pair of glasses for Gran.
Write a list of words to describe the glasses.

_____

_____

Book word count: 191

The Birthday Candle

1 What present did Anneena give Biff?
Colour the correct picture.

2 **"Wow! Fab presents!" said Chip.**
Which word means the same as *fab*?
Circle the correct word.

noisy

brilliant

terrible

3 Write the missing word to complete this sentence.

Wilf _____ the contest.

disliked   hated   enjoyed

4 Look at page 7.

Why did Biff's team lose?

Tick the correct answer.

☐ They got more points than Chip's team.

☐ They got fewer points than Chip's team.

☐ They got the same number of points as Chip's team.

5 How did Biff and Chip feel when they saw the cake with one candle? Circle the correct word.

happy   excited

upset

6 Why did Biff and Chip need seven candles on their cake? Tick the correct answer.

☐ They wanted lots of candles to fill the cake.

☐ They were seven years old.

☐ Seven was their lucky number.

7 Which words does the author use to show the noise the candle made?
Tick the correct answer.

☐ bang and pop

☐ hiss and fizz

☐ crackle and fizz

8 **An enormous flower shot out of it.**
Which word means the same as **enormous**?
Circle the correct word.

tiny

loud

huge

9 Put the pictures from the story in order.
Write numbers 1, 2 and 3 in the boxes to show the order that they happened.

☐   ☐   ☐

10 Draw lines to show what happened at the beginning, the middle and the end of the story.

beginning   Biff and Chip had a contest.

middle   Biff and Chip had their birthday cake.

end   Biff and Chip opened their presents.

11 How much did you enjoy the story and activities?
Colour one face to show how you feel.

12 Design a birthday cake for your next birthday.
Put the right number of candles on it.
Write some words to describe your cake.

_____

_____

Mosaic Art

1 Look at the Contents list on page 3.
Which page tells you about Roman mosaics?
Circle the correct answer.

| 22 | 10 | 12 |

2 Write the missing word to complete this sentence.

Lots of little _____ are used to

make mosaics.

| pieces | lumps | sheets |

3 Put the pictures in order to show how to make a mosaic.
Write numbers 1, 2 and 3 in the correct boxes.

4 Look at page 9.
What happens after the artist has stuck
all the pieces on to the mosaic?
Tick the correct answer.

☐ She hangs up the mosaic straight away.

☐ She lets the mosaic dry.

☐ She covers the mosaic in water.

5 Which words have the same meaning?
Draw lines to match the words.

little   organise

piece   small

sort   bit

6 **This mosaic has been made on 163 steps!**
Why has the author used an exclamation mark (!) here?
Circle the correct answer.

to show it is surprising   to show it is loud

to show it is a joke

7 Look at pages 14 to 15.
Draw lines to match the mosaic pictures to where they are on the steps.

the sun

the fish in the sea

the land

bottom

middle

top

8 How many pieces were used to make the bench in the mosaic park?
Circle the correct answer.

twenty

millions

hundreds

9 Look at page 18.

Why do you **Sort the bits** before sticking them to your picture?

Tick the correct answer.

☐ So that you use the right colours in the right places.

☐ It is fun to sort things.

☐ You can only use three different colours in a mosaic.

10 Look at page 20.

Which word means the same as *junk*?

Circle the correct word.

shells

rubbish

food

11 How much did you enjoy the book and activities?
Colour one of the faces to show how you feel.

12 Draw a mosaic picture you could make using different foods.
Label the different foods.

Book word count: 195

The Mosaic Trail

1 Write the missing word to complete the sentence.

material   picture   building

A mosaic is a _____ made with

lots of small pieces.

2 Look at page 5. **"How odd!" said Biff.**
Why has the author used an exclamation mark (!) here?
Circle the correct answer.

to show Biff is surprised   to show Biff is upset

to show Biff is shouting

3 Why did Chip say the little red bits were a trail?
Tick the correct answer.

☐ The bits went on and on.

☐ There were only a few bits.

☐ He saw who had dropped the bits.

4 Who did Biff and Chip meet first?
Circle the correct picture.

the robbers

**the man making
the mosaic**

the Romans

5 Why did the man ask the Romans for help?
Tick the correct answer.

☐ The Romans were better at running than the man.

☐ The Romans had horses that could catch up with the robbers.

☐ The Romans needed the mosaic pieces.

6 What was the man going to use the red bits for?
Circle the correct answer.

to make a trail

to make a wagon

to make a mosaic floor

7 How did they find the man's wagon?
Tick the correct answer.

☐ The thieves brought it back.

☐ They used the magic key to find it.

☐ They followed the trail of the red bits.

8 What did Biff and Chip use to collect the red bits in?
Circle the correct picture.

9 Draw lines to match the words to their meanings.

trail   a wooden cart with four wheels

wagon   a picture of how to do something

plan   a path of objects left by someone

10 Put the pictures from the story in order.
Write numbers 1, 2 and 3 in the boxes to show the order that they happened.

11 How much did you enjoy the story and activities?
Colour one face to show how you feel.

12 Draw a plan for a mosaic picture.
Write some words to describe your picture.

_____

_____

Plants for Dinner

1 Which symbol is used to show plants that you can eat?
Tick the correct answer.

2 Look at the Contents list on page 3.
Which page tells you about plant seeds?
Circle the correct answer.

18   16

8   14

3 Look at page 7.
Which plant has a root that you can eat?
Circle the correct answer.

4 Which words have opposite meanings?
Draw lines to match the words.

long   thick

thin   stiff

soft   short

5 Look at pages 12 to 13.
Which part of a broccoli plant can you eat?
Circle the correct answer.

seed   root   flower bud

6 Which flower smells **horrid**?
Circle the correct answer.

7 Write the missing word to complete this sentence.

A cucumber is a _____

because it contains seeds.

| vegetable | fruit | salad |

8 Look at page 17.
Why has the author used labels?
Tick the correct answer.

fruit with seeds

◻ to show that a new section is starting

◻ to tell us what is in the picture

◻ to show words that are in the glossary

◻ to show which plants you can eat

9 Draw lines to match each part of the plant with the correct sentence.

flower

> This goes down into the soil.

seed

> This grows into a new plant.

root

> This grows from a bud.

10 Which parts of plants can you eat?
Tick the correct answer.

☐ You can only eat plant roots.

☐ You can only eat the fruit from plants.

☐ You can only eat the leaves and seeds from plants.

☐ You can eat the roots, leaves, seeds, shoots, buds and fruit from different plants.

11 How much did you enjoy the book and activities? Colour one of the faces to show how you feel.

12 Draw a picture of your favourite plant from the book. Add labels to show the different parts of the plant.

Book word count: 202

The Stinky Plant

1 Write the missing word to complete the sentence.

animals   insects   birds

Wilf says that _____ like the smell of flowers.

2 Look at page 6.
Why did the man look unhappy?
Circle the correct answer.

He was bored.   He was lost.

He could not find a plant.

3 What is a botanist?
Tick the correct answer.

☐ someone who paints pictures of plants

☐ someone who collects and eats plants

☐ someone who collects and finds out about plants

4 The botanist is looking for a plant. What is it like?
Circle the correct answer.

It glows.

It has a strong smell.

It has sharp spikes.

It smells really nice.

5 Why can't the botanist smell the plant?
Tick the correct answer.

☐ His throat is sore.

☐ The plant does not smell.

☐ His nose is blocked.

☐ The plant is too far away.

6 Write the missing word to complete the sentence.

sweet

horrible

delicious

The plant the botanist is looking for smells _____ .

7 **... the stink got stronger and stronger.**
Why has the author used the word *stronger* twice?
Tick the correct answer.

☐ to fill space on the page

☐ the author could not think of a different word

☐ to show that they are moving closer to the smelly plant

8 Look at page 21.
What could Mum smell?
Circle the correct answer.

the stinky plant

the leaves

the flowers

Floppy

9 Choose a new title for this story.
Tick the best title.

☐ The Pretty Flower

☐ The Botanist's Big Nose

☐ The Sweet Scent

☐ The Pongy Plant

10 Put the pictures from the story in order.
Write numbers 1, 2 and 3 in the boxes to show the order that they happened.

☐

☐

☐

11 How much did you enjoy the story and activities?
Colour one face to show how you feel.

12 Draw a picture of the stinky plant.
Write a list of words to describe the plant.

_____

_____

Dressing Up

1 Look at the Contents list on page 3.
Which page tells you about film costumes?
Circle the correct answer.

18	16	14	8

2 Draw lines to match the clothes to the reasons for wearing them.

light clothes   to pretend to be something different

thick clothes   to stop you getting too hot

a costume   to protect you when it is freezing

3 How do clothes protect you in the snow?
Tick the correct answer.

☐ they stop you getting too hot

☐ they stop you getting too cold

☐ they help you to keep cool

4 Look at page 10.
What do the labels show?
Tick the correct answer.

☐ how to make the costume

☐ the different parts of the costume

☐ the author's favourite words

☐ how to put the costume on

5 Write the missing word to complete the sentence.

important   unlucky

ordinary

People wear special clothes for

a wedding because it is an

_____ day.

6 Draw lines to match the words to their meanings.

protect   a string of flowers

costume   to keep something safe

garland   clothes for dressing up

7 Why do some people wear red clothes?
Tick the correct answer.

☐ to make them feel sad

☐ to bring them good luck

☐ to bring them bad luck

☐ so they can be seen in the dark

8 Which word means the opposite of *special*?
Circle the correct word.

unusual   ordinary

different   important

9 Look at page 14.

Why do actors dress up in special costumes?

Tick the correct answer.

☐ to celebrate an event

☐ to keep them warm

☐ to bring them luck

☐ to make them look like a character

10 Which part of the book tells you what the word *carnival* means?

Circle the correct answer.

glossary

back cover

index

contents

11 How much did you enjoy the book and activities?
Colour one of the faces to show how you feel.

12 Design a carnival costume for yourself.
Label the different parts of your costume.

Book word count: 189

A Dress for Biff

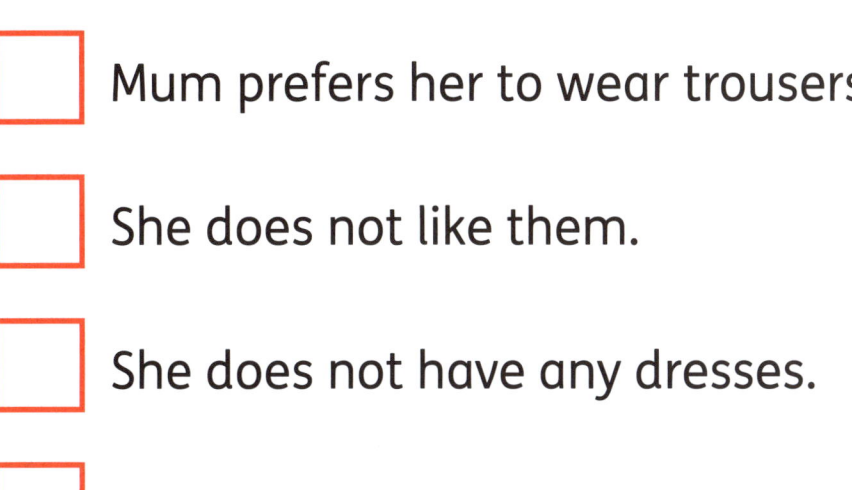

1 Why doesn't Biff wear dresses?
Tick the correct answer.

☐ Mum prefers her to wear trousers.

☐ She does not like them.

☐ She does not have any dresses.

☐ She gets too hot in them.

2 What happened first in the story?
Circle the correct picture.

3 "**What odd clothes they have on!**"
Which word means the same as *odd*?
Circle the correct word.

familiar   strange

comfortable   smart

4 Why did the boy say that the children's clothes were odd?

Tick the correct answer.

☐ The children's clothes were brightly coloured.

☐ The boy was being friendly.

☐ The children's clothes were from a different time.

☐ The children's clothes did not fit them properly.

5 Draw lines to match the words to their meanings.

guards	a king or queen's house
palace	people who steal things
robbers	people who keep a palace safe

6 Look at page 10.
What does the author use to show that the boy is shouting at the guards? Circle the correct answer.

capital letters

an exclamation mark

the word 'shouted'

a question mark

7 Why did the boy think the children were robbers?
Tick the correct answer.

☐ They were strangers and he had never seen people like them before.

☐ He saw them steal something.

☐ He saw them sneak around inside the palace.

8 Write the missing word to complete the sentence.

rain   king   guards

The children ran into the palace to

escape from the _____.

9 Where did Chip and Kipper hide from the guards?
Circle the correct answer.

in the clothes rail

under the bed

behind Biff's dress

in the palace gardens

10 Put the pictures from the story in order.
Write numbers 1, 2 and 3 in the boxes to show the
order that they happened.

11 How much did you enjoy the story and activities?
Colour one face to show how you feel.

12 Design a new dress for Biff.
Write some words to describe it.

_____

_____

My Words

Write your favourite new word from each book.

_____

_____

_____

_____

_____

_____

_____

_____

_____

My Badges

Stick your badges here.